(CREATURE SOUNDS FADE)

>> SHANNA COMPTON

Black
Lawrence
Press

Black
Lawrence
Press

www.blacklawrence.com

Executive Editor: Diane Goettel
Cover Design: Shanna Compton
Cover Art: "until the end of the world" by Kimberly Kimbro
Book Design: Amy Freels

Published 2020 by Black Lawrence Press.
Printed in the United States.

Contents

(INDISTINCT CLAMORING)

(ALARM CONTINUES RINGING)

"A closed caption, (READING), is stamped inelegantly on her forehead."
—*Reading Sounds*, Sean Zdenek

"The sagest time to dam the sea is when the sea is gone —"
—Emily Dickinson
1604 (We send the Wave to find the Wave)

The Eyes Have Woods — *wild, primitive within person*

The Woods Have Eyes

You woke with a line in your head
You tripped on a root realization

You lost the path deranging itself
from fact to conjecture & back again

wanting to go wild because of all of this thinking / conflict

You grew   hairy with conflict
through the evergreens

You wore a cape   inexplicably — *giving up on trying to be rational*
in the warm evening

The woods resinous   with amber terpenes
& something starchy-sweet like gourd

You didn't know where the trail led
You didn't exactly want to follow it

Renouncing

You forgot everything else
thorny, dark as pitch, pulsing

5

with the (MEWLING) of the mammal

snared in the loops

– Release your primordial animal
nature

of your chest

Names for Storms

I can't hear myself
for the (HOWLING)
several dozen states away

the wadding stuffed
under the cap
of the decade.

It's true:
I can't see my hand
in front of my face

because it's clutching
a stone in my left pocket.
An image of a windsock

at once fiercely & feebly
orange. The darkening
palpable. At the first

pelted drops we smell
the charge in the air
the same moment

we detect the quiver
in the skin of the dog
at our feet. The backs

of our thighs embossed—
a plush pattern of flowers
ganged up on the threadbare

armchair. The (BURSTING
OF GLASS) at each window
successive, percussive.

(A SILENCE EERIES)
between the (BOOMS
OF TOSSED TRASHCANS)

in the street. The (CRACK)
of a twig-snapped pole.
The (FIZZ) of the downed wires.

The television already
lifting its heavy feet.

Example Sentences

(RUSTLING, LOW CHITTERING)

The cedar apple rust is a oddly symbiotic
fungus, affecting only the cedar if it grows
on the apple, and only the apple
if it forms on the cedar. *Symbiotic*'s
not the word I mean. The gall
of the thing. It has, of all things, tentacles,
appendages known as spore horns.
After a rain the horns extend, hot orange
and gelatinous—alien even for deep forest.

It's gotten to the point I'm looking up
things I'm already sure of just to experience
the subtle shocks in their example sentences.
In the woods today I stopped to read the plaques
put up by the Conservancy. *I love the word
deciduous,* I confessed to the trees. The littered
spot where the stand of red cedars
once bristled unsettled me, crowded out
until choked for light. I rubbed my aching

horns. You're probably expecting it—
just then five white-tailed deer (CRASHED) through,
flinging themselves headlong, bounding
in arcs. My slender tentacles instinctively
retracted, my spores packed up and put themselves
budlike away. (ONLY-BIRDS SILENCE.) Only trees.
The autumn olive bushes around me
in the breakthrough sun exhaled, sweet and high,
like no creature on earth is able.

Aurora Says

Give me some light.
This galaxy wants to know
who you're calling ordinary.

Everything gets tiered
in a weird way. A dying star
gets ripped apart by twin black holes.

But there are others,
fellow navigators,
and lots more ripping to do.

Just look at us:
in this destructive process
we shine at many wavelengths.

(CHIRP)

Dark Acres

Who dresses up   as an image
That's no way to slip   into a mouth

Not ache-tired but diffuse   fading
in the tissues   of every muscle

Well—the world becomes   is reduced
binary territories   a progression problematically

spatial   The lids of our eyes shuttering
like insects kept overlong   in a malcontent jar

We attempt to predict every day's worth
to capture it and   keep it fed

Blanking in the sun   we cannot alter
falter   in a summer ripple so intense

it obliterates math   down to your favorite number
Perhaps a face will rise   for us here

a deeper deafness   a loosening of the inner organs

wearing upon an expression   some culminating word

(UNINTELLIGIBLE)

Barren of Pines

Inchoate   the idea that I'll have
something   to put down

to approximate the perfume
of eucalyptus   my sludgy operations

I'm a zoo subsumed   under a mudslide
A tossed trio of ships   rising in inkwell illustration

awash in bounced wavelight   Everything major
but the times I catch it   Seldom the intensity

of the rescue   a matchhead igniting
on the eighth   or ninth strike

If I could build a city   or thread a pasture with grasses
I'd admit I love the city   but confess

I love the grasses more   where thunder storms
rains flash   kindling at the ready

& here I go   pining for the end

Disenchanted Woods

(PINES CREAKING)

I sought and found
my father's grave she said.
Alas it is still empty.
Ghosts, bed, the last tangle
of the perpetual dream
she writes most nights
       each tremble as she rises
like the leaves of the quaking aspen
flashing silver. *I found in it*
a spiral of rope she said
a jar of chalk.
Around her in the trees
she heard no doves.
Alas she said
there is never a body.

Shorn Fur

My love I am a tangled I am choked & salted

My love I am feeling the itch of the buds soon to burst from my skin

My love I have emerged as a principal voice & I know you are listening
/ I'm making big plans to fix the end, to complicate as I clarify / Your
face is the forest

Your face is the font from which Thursdays spring amid freshets
of sentiment / your mouth like a deer hoof someone left hanging
in a tree

I trickle   a creek   when I want to boom

Geolocation's bounce   my signal glances off the nearest star

The wisteria down-dangles its bosomy fangs over the white lattice of
the bridge while the river rolls unperturbed, standalone

My love   might I breathe like a stand of oaks?

Pace like the beasts of the Middle Ages?

Bolt like the underinsured just after a crash?

My love I'm renewing to lock in my hot luck now / Ineluctable always,
each morning cinched like a belt, the aptest accent

Whatever you say, you cut a figure, my love

I will continue to snap your portrait, opportune

Tilt your chin this way   toward forever my love   my domain

In what world

can a person not
"have eros."
Everybody wants.
The haunts we linger in
fill up with (SIMPLE HOWLS) at times.
You must have been there—
the halls astounded,
rebounding our (VARIEGATED NOISE).
We sometimes exhaust
the topic is all. We dither desire,
smooth too many
of its runcled pixels.

The tip jar quivers in the steam
leaking from the dishwasher.
The glasses abound.
Another poet approaches
the spot where the mic
is not, sways as he quotes
from tough documents.
Outside we talk
about how we hate money
as we slip it into our bras.

Please touch our fur.
Under the mural
     the microphone alone
is both erosless & nonexistent.
     We've all heard the story
& we half remember.
     We've known most of this before.

Paper Trees

The picked edges of the birches'
bitter bark
      Red-gold admixture
of mind   a fleeting logical thread
she keeps tangling around
her spindle body

You'll have to look elsewhere
burdened   bent under the weight
of castigating hunger   She's mineralized
like wood gone stone

Her offerings   all burnt
into a chain of ash   She blisters
your vision   even after you look away
floats   beyond the divot
of her hothouse grave

Unassuming, the Kitchen Table (Plate 8)

List what you know.
>That I've begun in an uncongenial mood
a congenital statement
It's not like an infant's eye color
You can tell right away

Clear the table first, or use what's right in front of you.
>Larval stage   a pile of books
& the obdurate rubbish of household
mail, coffee in a green bowl, the drill & all
its bits, the leak-prone pen   Decluttering
the table just clutters somewhere else

Alternatively, look around. How far can you see?
>I can feel her eyeing me
across several hundred verses
of fictional ocean   The ocean's infinite, actual
but she's described it in an odd, flat way
For one thing, it's too long
& she shouldn't be singing   It doesn't work

Reduce, you pile of disparate functions!

      Go on ignoring the siren

It isn't difficult   When she changes songs

I adjust my ears   with a simple button

installed for this purpose   I could translate

or embellish them   but I'm not that interested

I have to   stick to the schedule

Closely regard the casings. Arrange them by size.

      The pupae have passed

from one developmental stage   into a group of words

that happen in relation   so we'll have to retrain them

as they emerge   The striations of their tightly packed bodies

reflect light   but not all of the light

comes from the expected angle   It's hard to distinguish

their color: somewhere between black & dark green

Someone has opened   the blinds & I

smell rain   I nudge the fattest, glossiest chrysalis

I'm not supposed to touch them

Arrange a dozen plates on the table.

      The eighth plate illustrates the workings

of the lungs   how they will inflate

the transparent sacs above her wings

Expect to see that by the third day

Notice the similarities & the differences.

The siren sings a refrain: *Close the book*

She's cheating   She persists with her plain, tired songs

They're all laments: *I've made many more meals*

in my lifetime   than I've eaten

& I am not halfway through   None of her songs

are new   to me

Choose one to break.

I think this one   will hatch soon

Brood VIII

(CALLING SONG OF M. CASSINI)

Your creature catches the scent of mine.
Both tremble, glossy carapaces
suspended in this dulcet vista
so ripe it looks painted on.

Trees titillate in leaf
& the irises arouse
their gaudy heads
to meet a warm soaking rain.

Let's spread out in this plum-
colored twilight, satiate all comers
in our shock-emergent number, shake
ourselves harder, if we have to,

when we go. Leave nothing behind
but the afterache
            of our racket   & a mortuary
of lace-winged husks.

It's trash night,

she said. *I'm taking myself out.*
It's been years since I've heard
the wild green parrots blurring
over the city & cried, overcome by
their misfitted lives.

      I don't know why I told you no
when I otherwise turned toward everything.

      Except I couldn't have admitted
then your possibility, misplaced
& wrongwise charmed,
no vagrant creature within me
resilient enough to insist.

Ongoing Experiment

I wondered if wonder   would reach a terminal stop
The tint in the air of the kitchen   in the first house

I remembered & tried not to   the odor
of the carpet in the apartment   I never had any trouble

recalling the green paint   soothed onto
the classroom chalkboards   I changed my name

at seven   I had some big reason, I guess
akin to the trees in the back pasture   hours spent

watching rabbits & knowing   too much
I pricked my fingers   with every thorn I ran across

assimilated rocks   from every dry streambed
My name became a glyph   I carved into things

but never said aloud   All these years later
I am the same woman   Taller & older

hungrier sure

(ROUSING CHORUS)

Sometimes we know the end
before we begin   get a chance
to steel ourselves against   or soften into
our disappointments
                      We spotted
a million budding elements today
but tomorrow expect one last hard freeze

Let it be kind   & final

                      Tonight no foxes
came (YIPPING) through the valley
though we went out into the field after dark
to seek them   & the cloud-ragged
full-on moon

Let it merely sweeten   the emerging green

I'd rather stay here & argue

about nothing   the way
we flick it back & forth   a netless game
Perpetually glancing   a battery
of tests we know we'll pass   Yesterday when the sun broke
through the afternoon   a verseless half-
remembered song from the shower   you asked
Feel like a walk?   I did but denied it
because I like the way you convince me
A creamy finish to the day   a recording in my pocket
of the spring peepers   (TRILLING) for mates
ruthless & demanding   in a temporary pond
hard-glinting   in the end irresistible
The females silent   claimed the naturalists
at first   until they learned to hear them

Substantial Atmosphere

Going sweet   at the sound *- Removing there*
of a certain voice   is a wrong turn sometimes *of doubt*

Let's wander into the desert   & do our best *- Eyes have woods*
not to wander out again   until we've truly starved *· but lot*

It won't take long   fellow animals *- fellow navigators*

Do you remember   the pale
then bright yellows of spring   when those still came?

Droplets of water   collected in patterns on glass
when we still had glass   to keep them out?

I remember   yet the clear, bald light
of the apocalypse   separates into rings

on the ice, too

(BREATH TREMBLING)

Buffer of civilization is gone, what differentiated us from animals is gone

Burn Pile

Under protest I undertake the task
unspecified except by labored feeling

What now must I regret? I purged
already once, only to wince

as you grew back. Turns out
we're inevitable, liable at any moment

to catch small fire & do what all flames do,
but for a hundred days in a drought year

so long it's lost its number
My resinous blaze, my ruined everything

I await as always the yellow appearance
of our next contorted seedling pines

(ORCHESTRAL MUSIC SWELLS)

An Obsession with Dirt, a Desire for Order

Here we travel among   all the warmer demolitions
We chase   the moderate harmony
into a third verse   of little-known lyrics

Ghastly   aren't we?
But concomitantly pretty happy   reorganized into
dweeby floorplans   hushed with shared shelves

Induce me to trade   my latest fig
Serve me any plain dish   I'll eat it
Tell me the prairie is studded with icebergs

No need to ask   I see them too

The general geographic area

is not impressed   you've finally admitted
its water's all gone   knew you'd never cave
until it did   & that every roaming mastodon
or rangy felid   died amid its thankless leaves
not once concerned   about your names

Double dose   pox   a fever settling into
a bright red ring   swelling when the skin
is pressed   Parched, the morning   Fetid noon
& I am neither florid nor ornate   I'm coming at you
blank again—   a plate dragging its edge
across the edge   of a neighboring plate

Logic, like land   isn't as solid as it seems
I scrape at your shell   as with fruit my teeth
I am not releasing or grasping   not reviewing, not rehashing
If what I enjoy turns out to be brief   & peculiar
I'll love it more   for its not being long or unstrange
Our guts are strung   & thrumming for the end ˙ crazed desire
for the end

Of all the planets in space   of every grinding chunk
of ice bitten to shreds   against shifting eons

we can neither know   or number really

how do I say this calmly—   it's true

she outdarks you ?

Like Rays, Not Like Speech

The good kind of tired.
I overhear people saying
    things they never said
stop to calibrate a few clicks
    get only (SQUEALING FEEDBACK).
I enter a loop   a slippage
    a few seconds catching
some minor traction
    before I skim loose again
The people mill
    about the room carrying
stacks of paper   illegible crimes.
    To the north there's a district
in which marble effaces
    the abraded effects
of perpetual lakeside
    fractured weather
in which the streets spoke
    inscrutably pointing toward
the city's shopworn past.
    Each citizen already
a statue. Every facade
    a fling of fancy   an acute
& sumptuous remorse.

Confirming Your Various Assumptions

Of course the animals are stone.
Of course the men are stone.
Yes the homes are stone & their doors are stone also.

Yet the animals are not stone.
The women are not stone.

The smallest unit of stone is the grain of sand.
No help.

Yes the cities are thunder.
Yes the streets among them thunder.
The fields beyond them raucous with the thunder of stars
    pillaging the unheeded botanical sea.

Rumbling isn't always in the distance.
A grain of salt. A single hair.
A fleck of ice.
No help.

We have outlived the thunder.
Outpaced the streets
    & somehow hushed even the stars.

Quiet, dumb stones.
Quiet, dumb doors.
Crack, stone men.

(FLICK. FLICK.)
No help.

At Mercy Meadow

Good morning stiff authority
I'm experiencing again   an occlusion of intent
As if every place is as blank   as an airport
& we're always waiting   to take off

Verbal the remedies   & hands like a million cilia
fronding   through the tenses
or the mesh curtains   hung between the towers
conducting voices trans-Atlantic   beyond the continent's limit

There are creatures   unlike us
who do better   They die without war

Every day it gets dark again   At the edge of the field
stand historical poles   skeletal among
the dusk-dulled hickories   still vibrating
all these years later   with the shortwave overseas calls

& a pair of owls repeat   their only question

Congregation at the River

Late hours roll in   sooty & untenanted
the ghosts gone wandering   Woe's plateau
feels plain   like no terrain at all

From somewhere   beyond the reach of this pale lamp
a pack stirs   hunched & canny   an evolving promise
not to spring   Do you recall the dark-

knotted trees we saw   across the river's broad waist?
How they held   a number of things
we made no sense of   until they fled

gray bodies spanning several feet   once unfolded
each neck an arrow   pointing resolutely away
Will we find them again   if we follow?

They say one's grave   is the simplest place
to find   You just look down

Seven Steps to Better Listening

We perceive difference
    where none exists.
In the exercise the green & blue overlap simply
    without true interaction.
On the following page the yellow block
    does not obscure the newsprint
because there is no newsprint—
    the layers are lies.
Likewise in the pine barrens
    when the red blur shocks bright
against the depths between the trees
    the patterns we think we discern
in the sugar sand are naught
    but desire. The inner violets
though apparently of two shades
    are actually alike.

(SINE SWEEP)

Seed Sink

There's a point in the sentence
where your voice sticks high.
You can smell it from here.
These tender-footed wildflowers
& froth of green are fooling no one.
You absorb the meaning of *snag*.
You already understand *windthrow* & *nurse log*.
You were born amid this tangle, ancient
with the light at evening, as imposing
as the leafless larch stretching its gaunt shadow,
a thrill all your own. You come upon
the tatty-furred corpse, the deflated
mammal you expected to find.
You can still hear what it has to say.

Sciences

Surgical   too clean
A wooded lot   vs. a wood

Where all is green in the eaves
Where all is pink in the panes

Contour lines nesting
in the deepening shades

It is the bile when she lays them
that makes them blue

It is only the (WIND
SCUFFING) itself against the ear

Orange into red   wafting
Green into blue   billowing

A pattern of rainfall
in an area already too wet

Set your embrasure for an arrow
or cannon   the woodwind your instrument

What if on that last day I refuse?   What if I admit
not a single science brings me   but several?

The Lost Sounds Orchestra

It begins to rain
    as if there's a thing
I'm expected to provide yet lack

I call out to my faint accomplice
    as she lies pale against the skin
of the moon glowering
through the open window:

    Trouble with the headdress?
    Trouble with the earpiece? Do you need me
    to zip your gown?

    I'm unfamiliar with this territory
where her expertise is as honed
as the flick   of a lash
    She only yawns at me   & smirks
of course she of course she of course she

Which course to follow?   The (STORM BURSTS)
    into the room   though we were sure
no one could find us here   stuffed
in a row of like rooms   (MUFFLED)

by leagues of asphalt   as deep
    as the end of the storm   as vast
as our improvised lament

Twenty Motels

In the first motel we'd ditched our parents
In the second we got caught
After a dozen I remember a green one   flickering
like a stripe on the highway   we blinked & passed

In the fifteenth motel I slept alone   but the bed
was crowded with grief
        & another halfway between two borders
north & south   three languages & every line transgressed

Each motel the set of a terrible play
The motel with stairs inside   so a hotel, really
The small squarish bed we laughed about
& the sketch I made   of you on the bus

The motel just far enough away   where the ice
from the plastic bucket   turned to runnels
along our skins   The one with the pool
at which all the lights ached   & I existed

as a cabinet amid a family   My sticky hinge
Every circular drive uncanny   & familiar
culminating in the handing over   of a key
The scent when you enter each room   the odor when you leave it

The perpetual abandon   abandonment of perpetuity

Each room breathing   like the spaces left

in a loaded sentence   On each borrowed bed

a suspect pillow   to which you can only succumb

Gloria

Don't pronounce any letters
I begin with none

I won't apologize
Like anyone, I was born

I heard him say: *The skin is unusually moist*
I heard her say: *You are standing too close—your breath*

    ∧

    (YELP) [. . .] I am the mouthfeel of transgression
           [. . .] I am the tang of glee
           [. . .] I am the grit coating your tongue
                  after you swallow
                  the contents
                  of the plastic cup
                  ∧
                  a measure

Each feather is so close-lying & fine
it can only be perceived
when you pluck it

No Contradiction in a Virgin Hero

It turns out she was adverbial,
a force to be first doubted, then believed.

Like Daphne, she could turn into a little tree.
Here is her mirror, with some tokens left in it.

The tomb exists, you know
though I have my doubts about time.

In her honor, I'm a hazard.
I'll be a plume.

Right under your nose,
a scrofulous rose.

A Little Instruction

Not having the least idea
what to do
in front of this altar

which must be the initial stage
Must it be   Latinate
obscured in a wreath

of smoke   Some things
leave us flat because they are
without piques

Paragraph after paragraph
nooses   aligned flush
with ideals   & prohibitions

Nothing's as simple
as a list   We fall
for them anyway

Inclemency

Batten your family & unfriend the unkind
    who wish foul weather on the south
Spite as obdurate as plastic
    We keep piling it into heaps
The ill-prepared & the deniers
    the harried & the lonesome
the men gassing up their generators
    as the children crouch & duck again
in hallways designed for the purpose
    tucked tight like that for thirty years
& when the power doesn't blow
    & the hurricane never comes
when the big ta-da reveals itself
    an overlong commercial for things
we all already own, who will turn out
    the lights without breaking
the switch   post the final comment
some incontrovertible word   dissolved solution
a miracle retort amid
our cast-off   blown debris

With Dashes Fitted, with Intent Spliced

In the salon the flitting energy pours
zero wedding riches on the flashes. For unity
we indulge in passes under every gable.
This for us is the same as *to seize, to call*, to talk
of "fountains of Tuscany"—transplanting apprehension
from one mind to another, one book to the next
in a gnomic microscopic hand. Yes, an elaborated parade
of our despairs! We issue again the shutdown command,
the (FLICK) of a susurrating blade. Think abandoned shops
dusted with the tracks of (COOING QUAILS), threnodic
as accordions. In cyclones we trust. Count the stuff
in these phalanxed warehouses while all babbles on.
We must align our quandaries & babble on.

Relative Degree of Unrest

She has none of my clenches
I need another page to work from
but since he mentioned the invading brain
algae I haven't worked up to the nerves
in my eyes   Baltimore writhes in the distance
& I wonder at my morbid possession   my position
that resides in the listening   She has none
of my flinches   my flung-off fluid
my extrusions of care   the wreck of words
I gather & preserve   *four pieces of jewelry*
two lengths of chain   a rain of coins
If the existence of   *hoards can also be considered*
an indication of   the relative degree of unrest
in ancient societies   how ancient
are we   am I

Misnomer

I couldn't write today
in the face of that bomb
    which makes me wonder
how we ever can   but talking
to ourselves & each other in poems
is a manner of coping

When I am angry that poems
do nothing   I am angry
& poems do appear to hold it
    I run over the brim of the bowl
I hold my arms out to the trashed earth
& all its frightened & ferocious people

— Poet's helping

Terrible appropriation of weather

I make no space for that man here
who means *biggest best most fantastic most lethal*
when he says *mother*   but he grabs my space
nevertheless   headlines   airtime   theoretical lives
he doesn't bother to imagine   spreadsheets
full of numbers   numbers full of awful profit

Trump

— forceful

I'm awful as a prophet   but I know
poems will burst from us   nevertheless

violent

Poetry will continue on

55

Contrast this sadness with previous meaning of mother

know that Moab was both brother & son
to his mother whose mother turned back
for a final look at the burning world   Maybe she
is the mother meant   Mother of bombs
Mother of brother-sons   Daughter-mother of a lot
of fucking woe   who burst as we burst . *Good people*
                                                                        Boeh

our damns   our horror   our burst in air

                                            MOAB

Reapplication / Take this word back

                    Affirmation - Poetry

56

Belief or No

You could put pressure on it
enough to press a diamond   buy a house or job
or you can let it breathe & filter you
as an alternate organ

It cannot unkill or unbomb
or right any of the earth's various
wrongs, though it can sound right
pretty trying   It can't hurt to pray

belief or no (no)   I explain
to the neighbor it'd take me a year
to fill in all these blanks   to amass enough
waste to top off such an ambitious can

& who has that kind of time?
In the early evenings I emerge to investigate
what unknown things grow
in our rented corners as (THE RIVER RUSHES)

presses diamonds from the wasted sun

The quality of the air

                    seems to be
improving   It must be illusion
Past-flashes provide world-built details
I put them in   because I want it to feel real
Because I'm consoling myself

This is where I get stuck
planet-body in decline   a mass of exhausted
stars flung   a double thread of light
looping back on itself   I meant every word

from that night all those years ago
till this morning   Everything I've said aloud
Everything I've written down   Everything
I've burned through   before it could touch you

Where the wall meets the river

Border Wall

the neighbors who begged it built are astonished

they can no longer see the river
taste it   sweeten it for the fevered child

Where the wall meets the river
the neighbors cease to be neighbors

they can no longer see beyond themselves
their hands in front of their own faces

Where the river meets the wall
the river cares not

goes on being river   thrusting itself against
all obstacles   carrying whatever needs carrying

She strives to be like the river

When the general gall threatens to leak
into my hoarded throat I remind myself

To have the same stoicism

the bitterness is on the public tongue
the salt sown into some other earth   not mine

I wore my dress

to the anthracite museum
where in delicate bushbean pink
all the chitchat was front-loaded

I wore my dress
I was somebody out larking
where in tufted titmouse gray
the minutes rolled by in wavelets

I wore my dress again
and again through the long garnet fall
where the beetles shone to each other
like glossed alphabets what grubbed under our speech

My dress wore me out
It made such demands of my saunter
through the strewn galactic mirrors where
I multiplied relentlessly against my best interest

My dress   my dress
o mess of shabbiness   o thread
bare habit   amorously wrecking
its own shadow

The Arson Prevention Program

It is exceedingly difficult
to come to terms
with the facts—
someone you love
is redacted

The river continues
as though no one
were missing

The country moves toward
violet abutments

ever adjacent
to the idea we
once had of ourselves
redacted

You must listen
to what's there
& to what's left out

You must love too
the silk & the must
of the ash

Everyone's asleep but the river

I wish you'd let me know
speaks all the languages   drills
above & below decks   Here's the deal
the contract goes often sour
& thus the house
yet the partners both apply themselves
to rebuild

Pls forgive this ungracious
& piecemeal way
of getting around Elizabeth said
in a letter
I ask you for same the moment I grant it
Not to mention the fine print
includes such circumstances

It is lonely in the bigass night, y'all
This is a moment we all common
& I'll meet you here
under my predictably blue light
wearing my best shadows along my nose
in this pile of other people's letters
readdressing whatever ills

Had I but
Had I but thought
Had I but done

The Vulture

You catch yourself
    first thing in the morning
saying *this is not a good day*
Prescience is a virtue   A vulture circles
over the river knowing already
you're late to your appointment
    have canceled preemptively in your heart
the possibilities that could have wavered
    in the pink glass along the far bank
the bridge in its green dress dipping
A world in which
children choke on gas & men posture
over them   The vulture settles
on a bare tree above the wing dam
surviving her kingdom
the only way she knows how
    preening her hideous head
You catch yourself
    first thing in the morning

(INDISTINCT CLAMORING)

White Chrysanthemums

This morning the cherries like sullen juveniles
   in the orchard amid the cries of other people's children,
but why should that be a sad way to begin? I don't care—
   why not admit the sun flatly shone with a too-early
intensity troubling every shadow like a doubted fact?
   Look at me, mimicking you. I cast my eyes around,
recalling yesterday, floating descriptions. What other way is there
   to begin when you're flawed in the ways we are? The lull
of morning, the lapse of afternoon, the throb of the day
   receding into the bath of evening, that sort of ache
I'm always proud of, but still—not a word written and nothing
   much accomplished. It is June, after all, with its heat
and persistent tart stain, its overhyped and rhyming supermoon
   I went out to see anyway, onto the county road
in my pajamas, where another woman in her pajamas
   had come out too, amid the glowing ghosts of moonlit
houses to see what all the fuss was about. It would make
   a good story to say we stopped and talked but
all we said was *hello*, then I came inside again, back
   to the small circle we make, like always. It must be true,
and it must be personal, I'm thinking, if I'm going
   to dedicate it. I can stall a bit and talk about how
it's the wettest June on record, how when we drive along the river

the gold-green blur of trees feels even better than
the water feels and how I pretend (or mistake) all sorts
of small unhearable sounds ((A SLOW HISS OF AIR) released
as skin cools) are audible to me now with my bionic
enhancements and poet's attention, though nothing
special is needed to detect his (SIGHS) as he drives,
the kind I worry about, or to recognize a few minutes
later the (LAUGHTER), bursting mostly from the chest, a (PECULIAR
EXHALATION), hard and sudden. I love this new-to-me
soundtrack and I suppose it's a bit mournful to think
about all the years I missed it. Except maybe
I'd never have noticed, had it not been revealed again after
a gradually accruing absence, in the same way the river
creeps lower week after week until stunned to roaring in a flash
flood that we pull over to watch for a while. Despite
the flashing alerts, there was no tornado, by the way,
and in fact it hardly seemed to rain at all last night. I slept
through it, rain being a different sort of soundtrack altogether.
Earlier I was reading back over the unfinished poems
collected in a folder, mostly half-starts and interrupted
sessions and noticed that I am somewhat stuck
on the yellow blazing of forsythia, letting it in every April
and every next April forgetting I've already said
whatever there is to say about the almost violent way it slashes
into the gray tail end of winter. But then!
the book falls open to "April and Its Forsythia" and I feel

not just forgetful but like a knockoff as well.
Anyway, the weather trouble never manifested
    and the peppers and tomatoes will be fine so I
am relieved (or deprived) of the regret I'd planned to feel
    for not covering them before I went upstairs to bed.
I've also been reading your diaries. We go to Maine
    every summer too, in fact the same vicinity,
without bothering to own an island. Oh let me
    dig: you're dead and so is everyone else. It's just
the envy talking. I wish I'd been there or could somehow
    visit now. Like our forsythia (but it is *so yellow*)
it's not a coincidence, the Blue Hill Peninsula, Penobscot Bay,
    memorizing views from Old Town kayaks (you said canoes).
I can see from the receipt I found tucked into the book
    that I bought it in 1998 so probably you did plant
the idea, because a year or two later I (lazy gardener) decided
    we *had* to go and we did go and keep going back.
Here's the brutal part about Frank, "the dead best friend"
    that wrenches but also makes me defensive (I'll get to why),
reaching to say something about my own friends who have died—
    and there are a few, but most of the ones I mean
are still alive, just no longer with us. Or I with them.
    So maybe it's me who died, back there in Texas
before we moved to New York, and then again in Brooklyn
    before coming here, and also all the practice I got
dying as a child, a darling Dear Departed, "oh look

at those dimples, will you?" I'm so good at it! A sucker
for all the flowers I imagine they'd bring. Really though,
    proper death seems way too blank and pointless,
so I'll never do it: I'll publish COLLECTED POEMS and throw
    a party on my one-hundredth birthday instead, a sucker
for the flowers I imagine they'll all bring. Turns out
    following your lead isn't as simple (I didn't say *easy*)
as I hoped, despite the way I feel as soon as I open
    your COLLECTED POEMS and start reading, sliding off
the pages into my own: for instance, if I had syphilis
    I'd definitely not put that in a poem so matter-
of-factly, not that either is anything to feel virtuous about.

    That's why those of us who are drawn to oceans and woods
are drawn to woods and oceans: we can be both intimate
    and at-large at once. Yes, and islands. Just last week
a man in a magazine lamented that poets were too much
    involved in themselves vs. the larger concerns of the world,
while here I have been sitting for years lamenting maybe
    my poems are not personal enough! It's a bit like your theory
(hypothesis, more accurately), that déjà vu is the lag
    of one half of the brain behind the other. Instead of
a schizophrenic tendency (as your friends suggested),
    just a simple synaptic delay or something—
you didn't explain by what mechanism—one half of every poem
    can't wait to divulge everything while the other half
not only lags behind but never even plans to arrive.

Once when I went home to take care of my mother,
who they thought at first had a stroke but hadn't, my sister
said (my mother told me) she hadn't realized
I was so caring. As if there's any other reason to pull so
hard, away! Here, I'll tell a story about when S and I
were first together, long enough for him to find my push-pull style
of love vexatious: he ran across some pages in a notebook
for keeping phone numbers that I'd incongruously used
to write a partial journal entry about another boyfriend.
He said he was hooked, entranced, a bit shocked too
(all flattering to hear), and since I was at work
scoured the house for more of the diary. I wrote a lot of them
back then and never thought to hide them
despite the dozens of people tromping through my house
each week, a risky parade. He found the box
in the living room closet and read every word
in all of them, probably thirty notebooks, going back
to the ones I wrote as a teenager, the ones I still haven't
worked up the nerve to revisit but also can't burn.
Before I got home he put them back in the box and didn't say
a word. He felt guilty, but also better. I'd been unbricked
a bit and didn't even know it. A week or so later we got into it,
such an argument, when we were still learning how! And he
said something he couldn't have known, no one could have,
and my guts shot into space where I felt them float
gravityless and black-cold for about a minute before

they slammed hot back into my core. I boiled the fuck
over then, didn't I? And I tried to stay mad, put on
    a convincing performance and hollered as long
as we needed to, to make our fledgling headway.
    After that there was no chance I'd let him go:
he knew too much and I'd learned a different kind of fear:
    not that of being revealed or judged but of the relief
I felt at being exposed. Oh vomitous intimacy!
    There's your Baudelaire's skull, I guess.
A constant ugly healing picked-at wound.

(ALARM CONTINUES RINGING)

The loops run simultaneously.

We grapple in the gaps   between the news.
She approaches   the front of the room
where the flowers crowd.   Every season
runs endlessly   finale-boom & cliff hung
until we're burned through   a flat-affect audience
blunted in the flicker   of perpetual episode.
Atavistic   our instinct to withdraw
to a safe distance.   *The chrysanthemums refuse*
to perfume. The chrysanthemums perpetuate
the rumor of themselves.   Resistance is
resisting   also this.

Sincerely under

a concentric deflation
—platonically—   meaning everybody
prefers the shadow   Happiness
isn't self-generating   but scuppered
on the sun-warmed shoals   Cubits, yards
whatever distance   defines
a combine will thresh it   as fiercely as I
cherish my lone vocabulary   even if
he recognizes my accent   A loose-curled
mum   droops over the mantel
We are here   filling the gap
of our own   enormous absence

Eager to lose her winter pallor

& the pensive demeanor   it nevertheless
graces like lace   on a mourning dress
She makes a cord of hair   to string a pendant
an inset of polished bone   We are all animals
No other jewelry   must be worn
the first two years   Black enamel traditional
for any loss   & white for virgins
pearls when the piece   marked the loss of a child
Upon the surface   sometimes a scene
of willows painted   with the beloved's hair

Immersive Experience

She had to laugh   It's not as though
some are & some aren't   *You're experiencing this*
all right   *Your ghost behind the wheel*
she said   *& several layers*
of plexiglass   Wake me
when we get there   or wake us both
a bit sooner than that   *Whose driving notion*
What's sustaining in principle   *How much*
for one of those Overarching Ideas?
I don't want to miss   the way we end

Leisure Isn't from Around Here

It's too far, she said. *I don't want to go.*
Her accent goes weird again
& everyone wonders where she's
"really" from. *It's too far,* she said.
I had to get out of there. Pleasure fails
to ameliorate every cascading pain.
There are waves one rides, atop
the toss like a secure & buoyant thing.
There are waves too though
that nurse at you until you're under.
Plush, the hush, an awareness
of its own, a sudden drop down into
the mote-filled light solidified.
Not a buoy, not a boat tossed,
not any seafaring thing. *It's too far,*
she said. *Already we should have
come & gone.*

The term for this is biological ornament

—an animal appears   with an appendage

serving only   a decorative function

Betray the ostensible   utilitarian

Ornaments   may be used to any purpose

Alternative theory: propose a center

the ideas   of quality or deficiency

the tones of mid-70s   filmstock entailed

Name your potential   Produce wastefully

extravagant ornaments   By 1982

we'll be advertising   diseases are a theory

& the hypothesis   is a new species

of cramping animal   Get a grip

on your beautifully colored plumage

before you dive

   It's late   & we're all tired

Even space expands with a (GASP)   Every light

fades a bit more toward wan   & we must choose:

elaborate / display / select / select / select

The descent of us   embroiled

with the scent of us   I'm telling you:

plumage   is not really the point

Galileo Believed Us to Be Seas

O lunar maria
O wrinkle ridge
Enthusiasm is its own spell,
                    switches

We have lain in long flowing rows
alongside the running water

We have plain tried even when
we were plain tired

Our losses are glossy
much-pitted maria
     Crisium, Fecunditatis, Nectaris, Vaporum
     the bliss-worn sisters

Cool as basalt
frozen mid-drift

Dropped Eaves

(OVERHEARD LANGUAGE), she remarked
like a character in one of her plays
about animals slowly turning themselves
into new sorts of animals. Someday
I hope we make it out of the wings
or maybe we'll finally get them
    enter a clearing in which
    we can see the moon
    & also catch a whiff of the sea
    as we feel our way up into
    devotion, a ready current.
Our problem's been obvious all along:
we're too tethered. Are you thirsty?
Tip toward me your throat.
A clear rivulet of water approaches us
across the sandy waste. Quiet now.
Keep still.

Science Fiction

It's almost too late. The mesa hulking
in the distance, ripe with sunset,
a sleepwalk away from Mars's ice.
Enter the state. Enter the temptation
to put words to unworded things, to temper
experience with a mouthful.
Heed the signs:
                    you cannot leave.
Are those black diamonds on your skin?
Do you feel an impulse to (RATTLE)? You
at the mercy of the matchbook. You
incubating in every proverb, named in none.
This skull-capped sky will never let you go.
This dust will dust-to-dust you, snuff you.
Landscape's misanthropic. It's never false.

High & Deprived

In the white space   of each page
a vision but   only briefly
In the white space   of morning
there is nestled   a sleeping
white space   I rose in the night
but found it inky   In the blank
that was filled   in the drawer
that was empty   in the open
in the nothing   where it stands
at the center of   a crowded shelf
the white space   occupies
all other space too   suppressing
& necessitating   the resistance of the rest
The negative jerks   the positive into being
The revealed letter's bowl   set atop the hidden stem
The point where   the sentence is pierced
by the tail   In the white space
between the words   & the banks
of the curving river   white clouds
not colorless   not impossible

I need a solvent.

You'll have to supply the variable.
In some places, the sun strikes
acute in angle
& everything gets tinged.
When your body is tired.
I've only got this one, you say.
Staticky & adrift in the regulating
push-pull of muscle. The slack
unknown to bone.
I borrow your pen & return it.
I borrow a book & forget.
I'll tell you tonight & tomorrow
& again the day after that.

Trick Ending

He had given me a necklace I think.
I held it fast-tight through a lull
in the ozone. Night came on
like the end of a film, not at all
what we expected, black-rimmed
& unreal the way holidays feel:
all the people different versions
of themselves, in different clothes.
We eat from different plates,
ostensibly finer. When I was a kid,
the woman next door unpacked
her daisy wedding china & served
a meal to her family on it before
pretending to kill herself again.
Perhaps she knew them kin to mums
& really two flowers in one, the trick
of the dogged dryad, a bruisewort,
a softener of sorrows.

Hometown

We are residue   the grit left

around the drain   as the rest runs through

& she is the ghost   of the ghost she was

that afternoon   standing in the hazel-

eyed field   behind the school

the sun   undiscerning

thick as gobs   everywhere

     I am the echo   of that afternoon too

& reverberate still   in this one

Each of us   stacks up like tree rings

We persist as words   years after

the speeches end   (RINGING) in our own ears

The Driest Place on Earth

Last place to be censored by
sea

I watched in horror as the man hung
half a pig by a hook in the window.

Nearby, the sea shone or something.
Nearby, the wingspan of a hawk cast an elongated shadow.

End of day

I listened with horror to the words I was missing.
A wrongness was growing in the living moon.

& nearby, the sea rolled endlessly.
Nearby, the sawgrass peered through the grit & preened.

I've never been to Florida. Louisiana however
is second skin of mind, a habit-habitat.

& Texas on the way there, the red soil
& black boars, the frankly haunted pines

lone men in pickups fishing
for nothing they intend to catch.

& nearby, the sea froths over the edge.
& nearby, the sea.

Nearer & nearer
the obliterating sea

final scene / very last stage of the end

A friend laments

that people do not really
want to be free
& she may be right

I watch the light
in its slow surge
from the tip of the park
& enjoy the dew
dampening my shoes
& damn my heart again
& all its inabilities

Hammer, I swear I will make this flush

When we attempt
to say vital vivid things
our vocabulary can feel
so thin in places
    a dress
showing too much of us
under the insistence
of the sun

You will have to trust me, simplicity

Trust me, directness

I am rapt in the aura of deep instinct

Memorandum pink

the magnolias are currently remembering
every last spring
    Fog clung as fog will do
to the hills over the river
in Owego
    I kept wanting to put an *s* in somewhere

I feel my mind like a burnished hive
acrawl with cooperating bodies
    All the colors of the last weeks
bled into a single stream
of light from the headlamps
    Every river we've seen
the same river

I'm chipper as dime store
but just as cheap
    I'm watching you watch me
& wondering how to pose
how best to catch & beggar
the brimming of the river alongside
unheeding us

Gelid   silver thaw

a gliding into sleep
        well that's for someone else
I'm a word on your tongue
coined geologic ages ago:
carboniferous
        Deaf like me
means I can hear even very subtle shifts
in you & sound has color the way shade
in the woods has scent
        Dominant land vertebrates
innate in us   *Which branch are you*
The person you are
standing upright in a glaze-event storm
        A body can be sufficient shelter
even at its weakest moments
of atmospheric density
        Cruel pixels
your heart is in the right place
but no mountain   no orbit's farflung parabola
no all-sucking collapsed star
could be more wrong
        You're an age
that must come to pass

the heating & cooling of the plates
the cooling & drying of the climate
      Glaciations scar every tissue
so we'll know   & grow them new

This isn't how   it's supposed
to work

& play suspicion   along golden edges

To represent   the journey
you'll need a stack   of pages

the time this trip took you   plus
all the days   you'll never get back

A blank   in every socket
a locket on a chain   glowing

at the edges   in a shroud
of dark enamel   In the corner

the dresser speculates   What comes
tigereye at last   coaxed open

What agate center   of us
rife with rhizomatic   lily of the valley

scented toxic   the last thing left

When is pleasure   a pressure

I've got a new gap   in my line
the way I feel things   sometimes instead
of hearing them   It's not easy
to explain   Speech is not remote
but a solid thing   that slips
& you & I   are both receding into it
into backlit space   frosted
& agleam   like galactic junk

(SOFTLY TRILLING)

The pond once   teemed with us
Alienation never knows   whose pronouns to use
We live under shame's grammar   accent grave
Yet dissenting   like the new shoots
that form in summer   from the barest
green of spring   so many buds
no catastrophe's   maxed out enough
to crush

Pale Cricket

A clear detail is a vague phrase.

A quarter is a phase of the moon.

Vagaries are not what you think.

The method is the statement.

I am tired again but find this reasonable.

I am happy to lie here in this bed.

I find satisfaction in the grousing.

The idea softens in the light from the bedside lamp.

The carapace of an insect in a high corner of the kitchen.

The (RATTLING GLASSES) in the cabinets as you walk the old
    floorboards.

The sound of you (TYPING) in the next room.

I've lost my verbs. The sound of me (TYPING) in this one.

Town of Horseheads

& then the town of Painted Post
Town of Bath
The towns sweep by,
nouns we cannot grasp

I begin inventing towns
that might appear beyond each ridge:
Town of Tables
Town of Nest Eggs
of Granite
of Poison
of Brooms

The Town of American Songs—
also known as Aching Plenty
The Town of Twenty Turbines
The Town Where the Sun Sank

Desert Valley in Bloom

Are we at last awash   friends & unknowns
adrift in the glare   inwardly   inhospitable
each lone star   an isolate smudge   of light
or as the prophet said   we're soaking in it

In the recent past   firemen combed the nearby ponds
as every commercial   flickeringly promised   everyone the body
part & parcel   of the Black Sea   Everyone who left him
in the street for hours   no vapor stranger   all red tape

a stranglehold   In the desert cluster birds   & the carton of Earth
yet (THRUMS & BRIMS)   with green   & eerie rainfall
Our poor cluster of void custom   We were no good as flocks
in among the milky debt debris   We overwatered & overpruned

& yet   ominously we put our petals out
For when the last flamingo   over the misplaced ice floes flies
& at last expires   she will note it in a (RAUCOUS SONG)
& all faint stars   their blue retire   in a streak rose gold

a gathering of tenuous strands   so heavily pendant
petal-scented   once civilized   once ours

(CREATURE SOUNDS FADE)

Threads   in your teeth
a sheet   in a rumpled crèche
partially wounded   loosed & pitted
one against the other   again
Breath left out   to darken overnight
Shake out   the pillowcase
Make a case   against against
I hook my curved bill   synchronizing us
back into fitting   colony
I crook my feathered neck   to muster
the vibrant color   the fleshy temperature
my dear-to-you   my (HOARSE-STRUNG SNARL)

Acknowledgments

Many thanks to the editors of these publications, for publishing some of these poems:

About Place: Desert Valley in Bloom

Academy of American Poets / Poem-A-Day: The Driest Place on Earth

American Poetry Review: The Eyes Have Woods; Congregation at the River

Barn Owl Review: A Little Instruction

Bedfellows: In what world; It's trash night

Bennington Review: I wore my dress

BlackLawrencePress.com: The Eyes Have Woods; Gelid silver thaw; Desert Valley in Bloom

Brooklyn Rail: Substantial Atmosphere; Memorandum pink; Gelid silver thaw; This isn't how it's supposed to work; When is pleasure a pressure

Bone Bouquet: Seven Steps to Better Listening

Connotation Press / A Poetry Congeries: Trick Ending

Court Green: White Chrysanthemums

Ink Node: White Chrysanthemums

jubliat: Disenchanted Woods; Ongoing Experiment

Laurel Review: An Obsession with Dirt, a Desire for Order; With Dashes Fitted, with Intent Spliced

The Nation: Where the wall meets the river

Open Letters Monthly: Names for Storms

Oversound: Dark Acres

Please Add to this List: Teaching Bernadette Mayer's Sonnets & Experiments: Unassuming, the Kitchen Table (Plate 8)

Poemeleon: Town of Horseheads; The Lost Sounds Orchestra

Sink Review: Twenty Motels; Gloria

Shock of the Femme: At Mercy Meadow

TAPP: The Arson Prevention Program

The Tiny: Confirming Your Various Assumptions; Misnomer; The Vulture

Typo: Barren of Pines

Women Poets Wearing Sweatpants: No Contradiction in a Virgin Hero

I am thankful for my spouse, Shawn Hollyfield, and for the friends who read these poems and wrote alongside me: Catie Rosemurgy, Becca Klaver, Rebecca Loudon, Elisabeth Workman, Maureen Thorson, and Amish Trivedi. Deep gratitude to Dara Wier, Diane Seuss, and Anselm Berrigan for taking the time to read the manuscript and offer blurbs. I'm incredibly thankful to be working with Diane Goettel, Gina Keicher, Amy Freels, and everyone else at Black Lawrence Press.

Notes

Some of these poems borrow words or short phrases from source texts, which are then used in a wholly new context.

- "It's Official, Gravitational Waves Have Been Found," Sophie Bushwick, *Popular Science*, Feb 11, 2016; "When two black holes merge, they begin orbiting one another. As they rotate, they move closer together and their speed increases until they are whipping around one another hundreds of times per second. Ultimately, they combine to form a larger, oddly shaped black hole. Finally, the new black hole 'relaxes' back into a spherical shape. According to predictions, this incredibly violent event should produce a type of gravitational-wave signal called a chirp." (Aurora Says)
- Bernadette Mayer's Writing Experiments (Unassuming, the Kitchen Table, Plate 8); "Attempt writing in a state of mind that seems least congenial."
- "Living" by C. D. Wright (It's trash night)
- "Concomitant with his obsession with dirt was a desire for order." is an example sentence in the *Oxford Dictionary of English* app, under the word *concomitant*, and was adapted for a title (An Obsession with Dirt, a Desire for Order)
- Mercer Meadows: Pole Farm is the name of a park in Lawrence, NJ, the former site of an AT&T transmission station that expanded the availability of international phone calls beginning in 1929.
- *Seven Steps to Better Listening*, CBS Laboratories/Columbia Records, 1964; the illustrations in *Interaction of Color* by Josef Albers (1963) were used to generate descriptive language, and one caption is paraphrased: "The inner smaller violets are factually alike. But the upper one appears to

refer to the outer lighter violet at the bottom." (Seven Steps to Better Listening)

- "not a single science brings me" is from "What Are Those Knives Shining Above the Seine" in *Où le bas blesse* (Where the Wound Writhes), *The Essential Writings of Joyce Mansour* by Joyce Mansour; the cyanin pigments in the bile of the great blue heron make her eggs blue (Sciences)
- Some of the phrases in this poem are grabbed from an internet search on "treasure hoards" (Relative Degree of Unrest)
- From "Stormy" by Jean Day (I wore my dress):
  I wore my dress.
  I was somebody out for a walk
  amorously wrecking down hot
  where she wants to sit in your shadow.
- The title is by Becca Klaver, stipulated in her guidelines for the *TAPP* flash publishing project; I borrow but rewrite the ending of this phrase from "Thomas Jefferson Inside" by Lorine Niedecker: "The country moves toward violets / and aconites." (The Arson Prevention Program)
- *One Art: Letters* by Elizabeth Bishop: "... please forgive this ungracious and piecemeal way of getting around to your book." to Joseph Summers, July 10, 1954 (Everyone's asleep but the river)
- The poem responds to *The Morning of the Poem* by James Schuyler, *Diary of James Schuyler, Selected Art Writings of James Schuyler*, and any quoted material is marked as such (White Chrysanthemums)

Shanna Compton is the author of four collections of poetry, most recently *(CREATURE SOUNDS FADE)* from Black Lawrence Press. Her work has appeared in the *Nation*, the *American Poetry Review*, the Academy of American Poets *Poem-a-Day* series, *McSweeney's*, the *Best American Poetry* series, and elsewhere. Born and raised in Texas, she spent a dozen years in New York City, where she earned an MFA from the New School. She is the founding editor of Bloof Books and works as a freelance book designer in Lambertville, NJ.